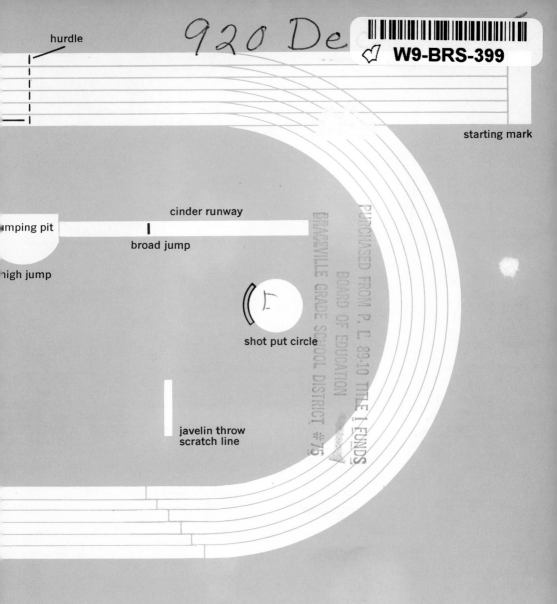

The discus throw circle is 8 feet 2½ inches in diameter and usually has a rim of concrete or steel.

Jumping pits are filled with sawdust or a mixture of sand and sawdust.

The broad jumper takes off from a wooden slab 8 inches wide and 4 feet long set in the ground and flush with the surface.

For hurdle races the hurdles are placed on the track as shown in the layout.

DECATHLON MEN:

Greatest Athletes in the World

BY ANN FINLAYSON

ILLUSTRATED BY GRAY MORROW

GARRARD PUBLISHING COMPANY
CHAMPAIGN, ILLINOIS

Sports Consultant:
COLONEL RED REEDER
Special Assistant to the Director of Athletics
United States Military Academy
West Point, New York

Photo credits:

Authenticated News: pp. 18, 56, 67, 76, 78
Free Lance Photographers Guild Inc.: pp. 22, 54 (top)
United Press International, Inc.: pp. 32, 35, 41, 42, 46, 54 (bottom), 68, 85, 93, 95
Wide World Photos: pp. 10, 11, 12, 14, 15, 16, 21, 25, 38, 45, 51, 52, 53, 54 (center), 63, 65, 72, 74, 79, 80, 81, 89 (3), 92

Contents

Decathlon Men, Greatest Athletes in the World

One by one the boys on the track squad jogged briskly out of the locker room. They squinted in the bright spring sunlight. As they approached the cinder running track, their coach stopped each one. Sometimes he would ask a boy to wait. More often he would offer advice.

"Uncock your wrist sooner. You'll get more snap and spin," he told a discus thrower. And to a sprinter, he said, "Work on your start today. You've been pushing upward instead of forward. You can lose the race right there."

He was a coach doing his job. He was helping each boy to master his special skill in track.

The athletic field was big. In the fall it was used for football. Now much activity was going on. Jumpers raked the landing pits. Three husky boys inspected shotput equipment. Hurdlers snapped their knees to get kinks out of their legs. Two men tested the spring in the long vaulting poles. Flat racers jogged gently, getting the feel of the damp track.

Finally the coach turned to the small group of athletes who remained with him. "You decathlon men," he said, "have you been listening? Everything I told *each* of them goes for *all* of you."

The decathlon men nodded. They were competing in ten different events. That was enough to make each of them a one-man track team.

The name *decathlon* is Greek, and it means "ten contests." The people of ancient Greece loved sports. They devoted much time to contests in running and throwing and jumping. These are the events we now call "track and field." They particularly admired an athlete who did well in many of these different sports.

The modern Olympic Games brought back the Greek ideals of sportsmanship and friendly competition. Men of all nations wished to honor all-around athletes like those the Greeks admired. So they introduced the decathlon.

The first athlete to win an Olympic decathlon was big Jim Thorpe, an American Indian. King Gustav of Sweden was host of the 1912 Games. As he gave Jim his medal, he said, "You are the greatest athlete in the world."

And Jim replied lightly, "Thanks, King."

But Jim's medals were later taken away from him, because he was not a true amateur. For thirty-six years after that, the decathlon remained an unknown sport.

Then in 1948, people found a new man to call "the greatest athlete in the world." His name was Bob Mathias, and he, too, was a decathlon man. Suddenly, the rugged, all-around sport of ten events caught the eye of the world once more.

Like the ancient Greeks, modern fans liked to watch one man succeed at many different events.

A decathlon meet takes two days. Five events are held each day. The meet is scored by a point system. Officials record each man's performance in each of the ten events. At the end of the meet, the points are added up. The man with the greatest number is the winner.

A decathlon starts with a 100-meter dash. The runners sprint about the length of a football field in one burst of speed. Bobby-Joe Morrow was the Olympic gold medal winner for the 100-meter in 1956. He once said, "Running the hundred is like flying an airplane. One small mistake and you lose."

But in the jumping and throwing events, the athlete has three chances to win. His best score is the one that counts.

Ralph Boston sets a new Olympic record with a jump of 26 feet 7¾ inches in Rome, Italy, during the 1960 games.

The broad jump requires a lot of speed. The jumper sprints down a narrow cinder track. He touches the take-off board with his foot and makes his leap. Sometimes he keeps on running in midair.

Ralph Boston, the Olympic broad jump champion in 1960, explained it like this:

10

"The style I use is called 'walking in the air.' I take three and a half steps in the air before I land."

The shotputter must have great weight and strength. Most shotput champions are so big and powerful that they are nicknamed "whales." It takes muscle to put, or throw, a 16-pound metal ball any great distance.

Another American in Rome, 1960. Dallas Lord puts the shot in the decathlon tryouts.

Inside a 7-foot circle, the shotputter cups the shot in his hand. Slowly, he rears back, focusing his strength on the shot. He makes a gliding hop across the circle. Then he explodes his power into putting the shot up, out, and away.

High jumping depends on grace and careful timing to clear the crossbar. The jumper usually approaches from the side.

Valery Brumel clears the high jump bar at 7 feet 2 inches.

He takes off from one foot and springs over. He must have great control over his body. Control helps him both to jump and to land without hurting himself.

Valery Brumel, the great Russian high jumper, practices weight lifting to build up his leg muscles. "Jumpers are like weight lifters," he once said. "They must be able to bring all their strength to bear in one quick effort." Brumel has mastered his art well. He stands 6 feet 1 inch and can jump to a height of 7½ feet. Very few other athletes can jump more than 12 inches higher than their own heads.

The rough 400 meter run is nearly equal to a quarter mile. It is too long to be run all in one burst. It is too short to be run at an easy pace. It is one of the toughest races in track and takes rugged and powerful runners. The 400 meter has been nicknamed "the murderous race."

A hurdler must be both jumper and runner. Champions at the 110-meter high-hurdles race must run with machinelike smoothness. They must sail over ten 3½ foot barriers without losing speed. Running the hurdles is like sprinting the length of a football field, jumping a fence every 10 yards.

Glen Davis sails over a high hurdle to win the 100-meter race for U.S. Olympic team.

Randy Matson spins the discus a record distance of 188 feet 2 inches.

Discus throwing dates back to the days of the ancient Greeks. The modern discus is a round plate of brass and wood, weighing almost 4½ pounds. The thrower stands inside a marked circle. Hooking his fingers over the edge of the discus, he spins to work up speed. Then he fires the plate out across the field.

The pole vault is one of the most complicated events in track and field. It tests an athlete's speed, power, and timing. The vaulter uses a pole for lift and the speed in his legs for power. He must sail over a crossbar, often almost three times his own height. After a fast run, he slams the pole into the take-off box. The resulting jolt sends him high into the air. At the top of his vault, he must do a handstand on the pole. Then he arches his body up and over the crossbar.

Cornelius Warmerdam, the first man to vault higher than 15 feet, says, "Pole vaulting is practically all speed. You need a body as hard as a rock to take the shock of the sudden stop."

The original javelin was a war spear. Soldiers practiced throwing it to keep in shape for battle. The spear in use today is about 8½ feet long. This is about the

Cornelius Warmerdam, great pole vaulter of the 1940's, soars to 15 feet ⅛ inch.

Robert Sbordone, javelin ace, hurls the heavy spear over 234 feet in the Texas Relays.

height of a room in a house. It tapers to a point at either end, and the forward end has a sharp metal tip.

The thrower takes a long run to work up speed. When ready, he draws back his arm and flings the javelin. It travels high into the air and far down the field. It sticks in the ground by the metal tip.

The two-day decathlon ends with the 1,500-meter run. It is 120 yards shorter than a mile in length. Men who make a specialty of this race must have great staying power. Many train by running 15 or 20 miles a day. One famous miler trained himself by chasing rabbits in the country. Others carry stopwatches to check how fast they have run a certain distance. All milers pace themselves carefully. They allow themselves so many seconds for each part of the race.

Don Gehrmann, an American champion miler, once said, "Every step counts. You must not run the first quarter one second faster than you planned. Otherwise you lose speed later on."

So, the young decathlon man has many heroes. He admires the control of the high jumper, the power of the shotputter, and the time sense of the miler. His pieces of equipment are as different as the long javelin, the flat discus, and the round shot. Decathlon men seldom become champions at any one thing. But they are often masters of all ten.

The goal of every decathlon man is to win the gold medal at the Olympic Games. The Games bring together the finest athletes from many countries. They are rivals but not enemies, and they compete in friendship. But each great decathlon star

This is a display of the Olympic medals. The young lady holds the gold medal.

does his very best. The man who wins this rugged event truly earns his unofficial title: "the greatest athlete in the world."

Here are the stories of two young Americans who won that gold medal and that unofficial title. Bob Mathias and Rafer Johnson were true masters of the world's most rugged sport.

Bob Mathias,
Youngest Champion

Young Robert Bruce Mathias banged the door behind him as he came in from school. Twelve-year-old Bob was in eighth grade. He had just been in his first track meet.

"Hi, Eugene," he said to his older brother. "I won the high jump."

"No kidding?" said Eugene, who was a junior in high school. He had also competed that day in his school's track meet. "How high did you jump?"

"Five feet six inches," replied Bob.

Eugene leaped from his chair. "Five feet six? You mean it?"

"Sure. That's only a little higher than my head."

"But, gosh," the older boy cried, "the winning jump in our meet was only five feet five!"

That was the day the Mathias family knew that Bob would someday be a champion.

The whole family loved sports. In his college days, Dr. Charles Mathias had played football for the University of Oklahoma. Later, in Tulare, California, he was the doctor for the high school teams.

The neighborhood children used the Mathias backyard as a playground. They played games or held races and jumping contests.

The four Mathias children grew up loving

sports. They liked to have contests and races. Bob's older brother Eugene was on the high school football team. Jim, three years younger than Bob, liked track best. Patricia, the youngest, was a fine swimmer.

Bob did almost everything easily. He was a natural athlete. At the age of five, he could throw harder and catch better than Eugene and his friends.

Even as a baby, Bob had good balance and good control of his muscles. He never

From left to right: Jimmy, Patricia, Mrs. Mathias, Eugene, and Dr. Charles Mathias, watch the family's most athletic member do chin-ups.

fell off chairs or bumped into things. Later, in backyard games, Bob often ran faster and jumped higher than older children.

"That boy is going to be a great athlete some day," Dr. Mathias said.

"Yes," Bob's mother agreed. "He is always so sure of what he can do."

And after the eighth-grade track meet, other people began to notice what Bob could do.

Tulare, California, was a good place for an athlete to grow up. It lay in the southern part of the great valley of California. This was fruit growing and farming country. The climate was warm and sunny. Boys could practice and play outdoors all year around.

At Tulare High School, Bob Mathias played on the basketball team. He also made a name for himself as a fullback on the football team.

He was a handsome boy with blue eyes and brown hair. He was growing up to be big and strong. At 14, he stood five feet ten inches. As a senior in high school, he stood six feet tall and weighed 200 pounds. On the football field, he plowed through enemy lines with ease.

But track was Bob's first interest.

Eugene said, "You are too high above the hurdle." He was watching his brother sail over the high hurdles. "Track men are meant to be skinny and light."

In Bob's four years of high school track meets, he piled up twenty first places and broke forty-one records. He was best at the high jump, the high hurdles, the shot-put and the discus.

Bob's coach, Virgil Jackson, was sure that the boy could become a great track athlete. Perhaps he could even win an Olympic medal. "Maybe Bob can try out for the U. S. Olympic Track Team in 1952," he thought. "That's four years away. He will have plenty of time to prepare."

After a hard workout one day, Jackson told Bob about his idea. "But in track," he added, "you have to pick out one thing and practice at that. If you're a runner, you choose a certain distance, like the mile."

"I don't want to choose," Bob said. "I like to run. I like to jump. I like to throw. Can't I do all of them?"

The coach thought a minute. Then he said, "Well, how about the decathlon?"

"The decathlon? What's that?"

"It's the event for a man who can do a lot of things well," replied Jackson.

The decathlon wasn't very popular in those days. Indeed, many people, like young Bob, had never heard of it. But when Coach Jackson had explained it, Bob Mathias rubbed his hands.

"That sounds great to me!" he said happily. "That's my idea of a *real* sport."

Coach Jackson frowned. "You have never even tried the pole vault or thrown a javelin," he said.

Bob did not feel the least bit down-hearted. "I can learn."

"You've never tried broad jump, either."

"If I can jump high, I can jump far," Bob answered.

"And what about the 1,500-meter run?" demanded the coach. "That's nearly a mile long. It takes a lot to even finish that race, let alone win it."

Bob grinned. "I can do it."

It was early summer of 1948 before Bob started learning the new events.

"Do you think you can learn the javelin and the pole vault in three weeks?" Coach Jackson asked Bob.

"Why?" he asked.

"The Pasadena Games will be held at the Los Angeles Coliseum," the coach said. "They will have a decathlon there."

"I want to enter," Bob insisted.

"I warn you," Jackson went on, "most of the others will be nineteen, or even older."

Bob was just seventeen. "Then I have to hurry to catch up," he said. "Let's go."

"Start with this," said Jackson, handing him a new javelin.

Bob balanced the eight-foot spear in his hand and examined the metal tip. The javelin felt light and strong. He listened to Coach Jackson's directions. Then he took a run of about a hundred feet and whipped up his arm. The javelin sailed through the air and stuck deep in the ground.

"Not so good, Bob," the coach said, shaking his head. "You need more wrist action. Try it again."

Bob practiced and practiced, trying to get the knack.

For the broad jump, he had to learn a whole new way of making his leap. For the 1,500-meter race, he had to time himself carefully. He had to decide how fast he could run each part and still finish well. Learning to pole vault 11 or 12 feet was particularly hard. He had to push his 200-pound body up to the height of a second-story window. It was a tough job, mastering new skills in three short weeks.

At last the day of the Pacific Coast Games arrived.

"Now, I don't expect you to place very high," Jackson told the boy on the way to Los Angeles Coliseum. "I just want to see how you do against real decathlon men."

Bob nodded. "Sure, Coach."

"Many of the others are college students," Jackson explained. "Most of them have been in a decathlon event before. You're the youngest, and you're really here to watch and learn."

"I know."

"Just do your best, Bob," Jackson said. "We still have four years to get ready for the 1952 Olympics. Now, you're on your own."

On his own, Bob proved his stuff. At the halfway mark, he had edged up near the leaders.

"Keep your eye on that kid," people in the crowd were beginning to say. "He looks good."

They didn't know that the last three events were new ones for young Bob, tough ones.

First came the pole vault.

Coach Jackson held his breath as Bob stepped forward. The husky boy checked his mark and eyed the crossbar. Then, holding the pole high, Bob ran toward the pit. Faster and faster he ran. The lowered pole socked into the box. Bob rode upward, pushing down hard on the pole.

"Pretty good form for a beginner," thought the coach.

Up, up, the boy pushed himself. As he neared the crossbar, he raised his legs and swung his body. The crowd held its breath as Bob sailed clear. Then he dropped cleanly to the ground on the other side. The young athlete's first public pole vault was a complete success!

As he trotted back for another try, the coach patted his shoulder. "Think you can push yourself over 11 feet?"

"I can try," said Bob.

He did try. Before the pole vaulting was done, Bob had topped a height of 11 feet 6 inches.

On another part of the field, Bob's whipping throw sent the javelin 171 feet. Then he finished by doing well in the grinding 1,500-meter run.

That clinched the decathlon meet. The boy from Tulare, youngest and newest of all, had won.

Coach Jackson could hardly talk straight. "I can't believe it!" he cried. "I just can't believe it!"

But his pupil had an even bigger surprise in store. "Coach, the National Championships are only two weeks off. I'm going to enter."

"You're going to enter the Nationals?" gasped the coach.

"Sure," Bob said. He had it all figured out. "The National Championships are also the Olympic tryouts. The first three winners at the Nationals make the United States Olympics Team."

Virgil Jackson stared at his pupil. "You mean, you don't want to wait for 1952? You want to try out for the Olympics this year?"

"Why not?" Bob said.

"All right," the coach agreed slowly. "After today, I'm willing to try anything."

Two weeks later, Bob entered the National Decathlon Championships at Bloomfield, New Jersey. It was more rugged than the Pasadena Games. There were men of greater experience and strength.

"Irving Mondschein will win," some fans argued. "He's been national champion three times in a row. He's even better this year."

Others disagreed. They favored Floyd

Wearing Tulare High colors, Bob puts the shot in the National Decathlon Championship events.

Simmons, a former student at the University of North Carolina. "Mondschein has had his day," they said. "Watch Simmons. He's the top man now."

Almost no one thought about the youngster from Tulare, California.

But forty-eight hours later, Bob Mathias was no longer a stranger. He had won easily over his older rivals, Mondschein and Simmons.

All three of them were chosen for the 1948 United States Olympic Decathlon Team. They would go to England and meet the world's greatest decathlon champions. There would be twenty-eight athletes from nineteen countries. This was not going to be like the Pasadena Games or Bloomfield.

Decathlon fans feared the worst. European decathlon men had far better records than Mondschein and Simmons. Experts put little faith in Mathias. "He's too young," they objected. "The decathlon is for mature men. It takes training and polish. It takes the strength to last. No raw kid has a chance in the Olympic decathlons!"

But one raw kid was determined to try. "I know what I can do," Bob insisted quietly. With his parents and his brother Eugene, he sailed for London.

He was the youngest member of the U.S. Track Team. He was the youngest person ever to compete in any modern Olympic track and field event.

During the first day of the Games, the temperature reached 93 degrees. Then the weather suddenly turned chilly. It rained. The track was wet and slippery. The javelins and discuses slipped in the athletes' hands. Practicing was difficult and sometimes dangerous.

The decathlon contests began on a rainy day in August. The rain didn't keep the

spectators away. Wembley Stadium held an excited crowd of 80,000 fans.

Bob's first-day showing wasn't very good. In his first high jump, he knocked down the crossbar twice.

"That's only 5 feet 9!" Eugene yelled from the sidelines. "You did nearly that well when you were twelve!"

Bob clears the bar
in the high jump.

Bob grinned and nodded and took another run. This time he sailed over the bar with ease.

Shortly afterward, Bob ran into bad luck in the shotput. The officials ruled out his best throw.

42

"You stepped out of the box from the wrong side," they told him.

"Nobody ever explained that rule," he said. He tried again, but his second attempt wasn't as good as his first. Points were lost.

At the end of the day, Eugene compared his brother's score with the others. "Bob is third," he said to his parents. "Kistenmacher of Argentina is 45 points ahead of Bob. Heinrich of France has 32 more points."

But when Bob came out of the locker room, he felt sure of himself. "Don't worry," he insisted. "I'll be up there on the winner's stand to get a medal. You just wait and see."

"Aren't you even worried?" his father asked him.

"Nope," Bob answered. "They don't give points for worrying."

Bob rose next morning before eight

o'clock and ate a steak. After breakfast, he and his twenty-seven rivals climbed aboard a bus headed for the stadium. Steam clouded the windows.

"The weather is worse than ever," said Bob's seatmate.

"Yes," Bob agreed. "We're having rain and more rain. The track will probably be all puddles."

"We can expect fog, too. We'll be lucky if we can see the scoreboard."

As the track men had expected, the cinder paths were full of water. More rain fell, and fog moved in. At times, spectators could see only the orange flash of the starting gun.

There were so many athletes in the decathlon that they had to be divided into two groups. The second group always had to wait until the first had finished its contest or race. Only then could the second

**Yugoslavia and Iceland athletes compete with
Bob, who wins this 110-meter race.**

group start. Bob had bad luck. He was in
the second group, while all his big rivals
were in the first. It was to be a day of
long, chilling waits.

The first event was the 110-meter hurdles.
Then came the discus throw. Bob made a
good throw, but officials lost his marker peg
in the fog. They hunted for more than an
hour and finally gave up.

"We'll award you 144 feet 4 inches," they
told the boy.

In darkness and rain, Mathias and Games Judge hunt for marker at Wembley Stadium.

A bystander yelled angrily, "Why, he threw it a good 4 feet farther than that!"

But the mark stood. "It can't be helped," Bob said to his family. "Forget it. I can try for more points in the next event."

He started for the pole vault area. In a raincoat, he sat down at the sidelines. While others took their turns, he just sat.

46

"Aren't you going to start?" Eugene asked anxiously.

"I'm waiting for the crossbar to get up to 10 feet."

"But if you miss at 10 feet, you won't get any points at all!"

"I can jump 10 feet."

The brothers watched the crossbar inch up, 8 feet, 9 feet. Slowly the hours dragged by. At midday, Bob ate a box lunch.

It was getting dark when the crossbar was set at 10 feet. Bob rose. "Well, here goes," he said.

It was raining again. Bob could not see the crossbar. Officials marked the edge of the vaulting pit with a white sneaker. But Bob made the vault with room to spare.

Eugene breathed a sigh of relief. "At least he didn't lose all those points," he said to Dr. and Mrs. Mathias. Bob's final vault was nearly 11½ feet.

At suppertime, Mrs. Mathias tried to get Bob to eat, but he shook his head. "I'm too tired," he said.

"There are only two events left," Eugene said, hoping to make Bob feel better.

Bob nodded. "And I need another 762 points just to tie for first place." He picked up his javelin. He would have to throw the spear as never before.

Floodlights had been turned on, but fog made them dim. "Where's the foul line?" Bob asked an official.

"I'll mark it with a flashlight," the man answered.

Bob took off in a smooth run. At the mark, he swung his arm. The javelin went whistling into the darkness. Down the field, an official marked its fall.

Out of the darkness came an excited voice: "That's 31 feet farther than the Frenchman!"

Only one event remained—the 1,500-meter run. It was ten-thirty at night. Most spectators had given up and gone home. But excitement was beginning to grip those who stayed.

"Come on, Tulare!" yelled an American from the stands.

"The kid's going to do it!" a man cried. "Just another 200 points, and he'll have it!"

On the track, Bob took his mark and waited. Then he tensed. The starting gun banged. Bob took off on his final effort.

"You can do it!" he heard someone yell. "Come on, Bob! Come on!"

The boy from Tulare was worn out from his long, hard day. His tired muscles ached. He was cold and wet. But he kept going.

He was almost staggering as he crossed the finish line. His parents were there. "Oh, Mom, I'll never try this again!" he gasped. Then his legs gave way.

But Mrs. Mathias knew her son better than that. "Listen to what they're saying on the public-address system," she said.

"First place in the decathlon," came the voice of the announcer, "goes to R. B. Mathias, United States of America."

Bob Mathias had done what no one had done before. He had won the Olympic decathlon medal at the age of seventeen. And by doing so, he had given new importance to this ancient but neglected sport.

Bob gradually got his breath back. "Well, maybe I will try it again in 1952," he said, eyes glowing. "Maybe I'll be rested up by then."

The following day, young Robert Bruce Mathias waited for his medal on the stand. It was bright and sunny again. The stadium was crowded once more. While the band played "The Star-Spangled Banner,"

Bob Mathias, youngest
Olympic Decathlon
champion.

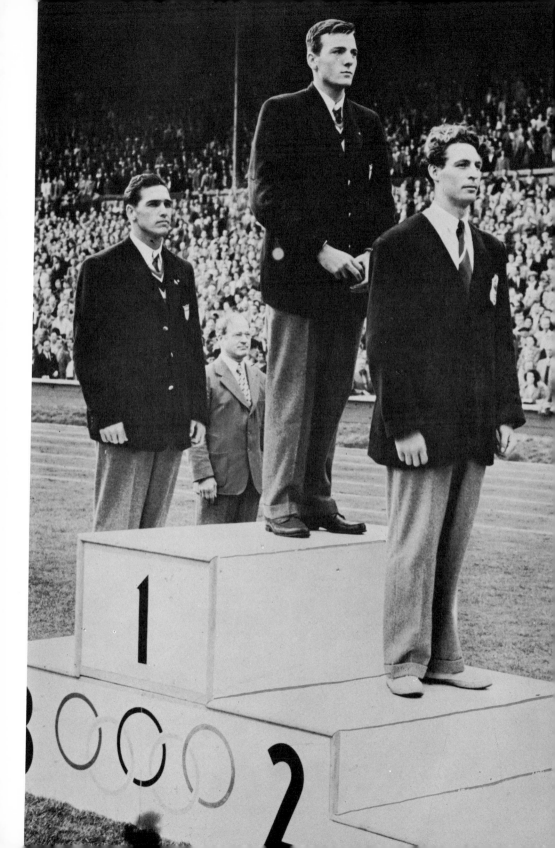

Bob Mathias, star fullback at Stanford, carries the ball for a big gain.

a ribbon was hung around Bob's neck. On the end of the ribbon was the gold medal.

Bob looked down at it, the roars of the crowd in his ears. He knew he would be back in 1952.

Back in the United States, Bob went to college. At Stanford, where he studied to be a coach, he played fullback on the football team. He played in the Rose Bowl championship game one year.

But his real love was track and field, particularly the decathlon. The sport had suddenly become popular. Tulare was filled with youngsters learning the events of the decathlon. All over America, all over the world, people were thinking and talking about it.

Crowds in Tulare turned out to give Bob a rousing welcome home.

"Why should I be only a runner or a jumper?" young athletes asked themselves. "Why not be an all-around champion?"

Later, Bob Mathias went on to win other decathlon awards. He was U. S. National Champion four times. He also won the Scandinavian championships in 1949 and the Swiss National in 1950. He won every decathlon meet he entered. And at the 1952 Olympic Games in Helsinki, Finland, he won again. He broke his own 1948 record for the decathlon. He did better in every single event than he had four years before. He is the only athlete who has twice won an Olympic gold medal for this rugged event.

But Bob Mathias had been at his greatest on that wet, cold night in London. Young and alone, giving his best, he had shown the world a new idea of sport.

Rafer Johnson, Hard-Working Champion

"I couldn't beat Mathias, at least not yet. But I bet I could beat all those others."

The high school boy and his track coach were watching a decathlon meet. It was the first the boy had ever seen. The coach smiled at his pupil's serious tone. "You really think you could beat all those others?" he asked.

"Yes, sir," the boy answered. "And if I work hard, maybe someday I'll even do better than Mathias himself."

"You'll do better than Mathias? Why, he's an Olympic champion!"

"I can be an Olympic champion, too, someday," replied Rafer Lewis Johnson. "It may take four or five hours of practice every day. But I don't mind work."

Rafe Johnson had never minded work. Even as a little boy, he had been bursting with energy.

Rafe was born in Texas, the second of five children. His family lived in an all-Negro section of Dallas. Life was very hard there. Negroes were denied good schools, good jobs, good homes.

"Elma," Mr. Johnson said to his wife one day, "there's no future for these kids in Texas. Let's move."

Rafe's mother sighed. "But where can we move, Lewis? It seems as if nobody wants people like us."

"California is a land of opportunity,"

Mr. Johnson replied. "And they have fine schools out there. I want my children to have good educations."

At length Mrs. Johnson agreed to try California. When Rafer was nine, the family moved to Kingsburg, a small town not far from Tulare.

Times were hard for the Johnsons in California. Their first home was an old railroad boxcar. It stood on a side track, rusty and deserted. A ragged curtain divided the inside into two rooms. Here the seven members of the Johnson family slept, cooked, and ate their meals.

Prejudice, too, followed them to Kingsburg. Narrow-minded neighbors called them names. Mr. Johnson's boss, Edward Fishel, was told to fire Rafe's father. Mrs. Johnson herself was threatened.

"Get out of town, if you know what's good for you," she was told.

The younger children, Erma and Delores, started crying. Their mother comforted them as best she could, but she was worried too. When her husband came home from work, she told him what had happened. "Maybe we ought to move, Lewis," she said. "Maybe it isn't safe for the children."

But Lewis Johnson liked California and was sure that his family had a future in Kingsburg. "I didn't leave Texas just to be pushed around again," he said to his wife and sons. "We're going to stay here, and we're going to make good."

Mr. Fishel stood by the Johnsons. He kept Lewis on and found Mrs. Johnson a job, too. He even found a small house for the family.

Little by little, life grew better. Even with his parents working, the family was very poor. Often Rafe and his brothers had to pick fruit for nearby farmers.

Rafe was always up and ready to go at dawn. "Come on, get up!" he would urge his sleepy brothers. "We've got to get out there and pick that fruit!"

"That Rafe," grumbled one brother. "He can pick three baskets of fruit while I'm still waking up."

Later at Kingsburg High School, Rafe put just as much energy into athletics.

"That Rafe Johnson," his classmates marveled. "He scores more points than anybody else on the basketball court."

"That Rafe Johnson," said townspeople. "Did you see him carry the football on that long end run?"

"That Rafe Johnson," complained the principal of Kingsburg High. "I know our team needs a power hitter. But does Rafe have to break all the bats?"

But what Rafe liked best was track. Coach Murl Dodson was amazed at the

Young Rafe is taking a practice run. Coach Murl Dodson holds the stopwatch.

boy's speed and the way he could jump and throw. So, one day, he drove Rafe to Tulare, 25 miles away. Together, they watched Bob Mathias compete in the decathlon.

That day Rafe decided he wanted to become an Olympic champion. He started practicing long, hard hours. The work paid off. Just four weeks later, he entered his first decathlon meet and won.

The people of Kingsburg were so proud of their hometown boy that they almost burst. "Rafe," they said, "we want you to compete in the National Championships. We've taken up a collection to pay your expenses to Atlantic City, New Jersey. What do you say?"

Rafe's thoughts went back to that day when other Kingsburg people had come to the Johnson house. They had felt hatred for Rafe's family. He could remember his father's voice saying, "We're going to stay here, and we're going to make good." And they had. By sticking it out they had won the respect of their neighbors.

Rafe smiled back at his friends and replied, "Thank you very much. I'll certainly do my best."

Rafe did do his best at Atlantic City. But he did not win the National Championship. He came in third.

"That's pretty good," his coach said, trying to cheer him up. "Third in the Nationals is pretty good."

Rafe shook his head stubbornly. "Only first place is good enough. I'm going to be first in the Nationals. And then I'm going to be first at the Olympic Games."

Another year of hard work followed. Then, in the summer of 1955, Rafe won first place in the decathlon at the Pan-American Games in Mexico City.

In Mexico City, Rafe puts the shot over 44 feet during 1955 Pan-American Games.

The town of Kingsburg went wild with excitement. When Rafe returned home, people held a special track meet in his honor. There, in his own home town, Rafe broke the world's decathlon record.

Excited Mrs. Johnson hugged her tall son. "You're the best in the whole world, Rafe!"

"No, Mom," Rafe said. "I won't be the best in the world until I place first at the Olympic Games."

Many colleges wanted Rafe as a student and to play on their teams. He chose the University of California at Los Angeles.

The football coach wanted Rafe to come out for practice. "You could make the varsity squad easily," he said.

But the Kingsburg boy had other plans. "I'm going all out for track, Coach," he said. "I want to give every minute I can to that."

At U.C.L.A., Rafe practices javelin throwing.

At college, Rafe Johnson went all out for a lot of things. He was very popular with his fellow students. They invited him to join a fraternity and three honor groups. Between his classes and his club duties, he attended meetings of six committees and sang in two church choirs. Still, he managed decathlon practice four, five, and sometimes six hours a day.

"That Rafe Johnson," his friends said, "doesn't he ever get tired?"

In spite of injuries, Rafe takes first place in the National Championships of 1956.

In July 1956, Rafe entered the National Decathlon Championships at Crawfordsville, Indiana. The three winners at this meet would be named as the United States Olympic Decathlon Team.

During the first day of the meet, Rafe hurt his knee high jumping. The following day, while throwing the discus, he twisted it again. The injury kept him from breaking his own record, but it did not keep him from coming in first and winning a place on the Olympic team.

"Johnson will take the Olympic gold medal this fall," everyone agreed.

It was Rafe's dream. Ever since he had seen that decathlon meet in Tulare, he had worked toward a place on the Olympic team. Now, he was not only on the team, he held two places. He had made the team as a broad jumper as well as a decathlon man. He practiced harder than ever.

Rafe was in good spirits as the Games began. But then the knee he had injured at the Nationals began to hurt. "I guess I'd better drop out of the broad jump," he told the track coach sadly.

"How do you feel about dropping out of the decathlon?" his coach asked. "After all, that's much more demanding than the broad jump."

"No," Rafe insisted, "the decathlon is my sport. I'm sure I can make it."

So Rafe practiced, trying to ignore the pain in his leg. It hurt so much that he leaned more heavily on his other leg. That put him off balance. As he landed from a jump one day, a new pain shot through his body.

Rafe rolled over, holding his side. Coaches and trainers came running. "What is it, Rafe? Are you hurt?"

With help, Rafe limped off the field.

In the dressing room, he was examined. He had pulled a muscle. "Just strap it up tight," he told the coach.

Coaches and teammates exploded. "This is your second injury!" they cried. "You can't hope to win now!"

It was true, Rafe knew. Two injuries would keep him from winning. He couldn't possibly defeat the world's best decathlon men.

Then Rafe looked down at the United States emblem on his track suit. "I'm competing for my country," he said. "I've got to do my best—win, lose, or draw."

And he did. Despite the pain of his two injuries, Rafe Johnson took part in the decathlon.

He was one-tenth of a second behind big Milt Campbell of Plainfield, New Jersey, in the 100-meter dash. He won the broad jump. But the strain was beginning to tell.

His shotput fell several feet short of his usual mark. He could not put quite enough spring into his high jumping. By the time for the pole vault, Milt Campbell was leading by over 600 points.

But Campbell missed his vault at a fairly low height. Hopefully, Rafe kept on jumping, although every try put further strain on his injuries. He closed the gap between them to less than 400 points.

Rafe adds some points to his score with an outstanding performance in the pole vault at the Olympic Games of 1956.

But that was not enough. When the final event came, Rafe knew his dream was not going to come true.

The men lined up for the 1,500-meter run. Rafe thought, "Second place isn't what I want. But it's better than third or fourth. One U.S. athlete is going to win the gold medal. So, an American is going to win the silver, too."

The starting gun went off. Rafe drove his painful muscles into one last effort. He was going to run the best 1,500-meter race of his life.

There was the finish line. He burst across it, knowing that he had won second place. As the runners slowed down, Rafe was the first to reach Milt Campbell.

"You did a wonderful job," he panted. He put his arm around the New Jersey boy's shoulders. "You deserved to win the gold medal."

The 1956 Olympic Decathlon winners: (left to right) Rafer Johnson, Milton Campbell, and Vasily Kuznetsov.

Campbell knew how much his rival had wanted that gold medal. "Thanks, Rafe," he said. "And you were pretty terrific yourself."

In spite of his weariness and his injuries, Rafe managed a smile. "I'll be back in 1960. Maybe then it will be a different story."

"I hope so, Rafe," said Campbell seriously. "I sure do hope so."

Back home, Rafe's injured leg was operated on. While he was resting he did some serious thinking about his life. Until then, he had not decided on the career he wanted to follow.

"I like sports, and I like people," he told his college adviser. "Isn't there a way I can put the two together?"

"You could teach athletics," the professor suggested. "Many schools need good coaches. A good coach can do a lot for youngsters."

Rafe liked the idea. He thought of many great Negro athletes. In track alone, there were such great names as Jesse Owens, Harrison Dillard, Ralph Boston, Wilma Rudolph, and many others. All had been helped at some time or other by their coaches. All had been trained, advised, given a start by teachers. Rafe himself owed a lot to his high school and college coaches. Yes, Rafe liked the idea.

He switched to a physical education course. In practice classes, he worked with youngsters. Many of them were Negro children from poor families. They reminded him of his own hard childhood.

"Gee, I'll never do it right," cried a youngster one day. He dropped his shot in disgust and started to leave the field.

"Come back here, son!" Rafer called after him. "Now, what's the idea of walking out like that?"

Rafe listens while Elvin Drake, track coach at U.C.L.A., gives him some good advice.

The boy hung his head. "I just can't do it," he muttered. "I'm no good at it. I'll have to try something else."

"How do you know you're not good?" Rafe demanded. "You gave up after the first try."

"It's easy for you to say," the boy grumbled. "You're a champion."

"You think it's easy to be a champ?" Rafe said. "It isn't easy at all. It's hard work. In fact, in anything you try, it's hard work to get to the top."

Then the tall athlete laughed and patted the boy's shoulder. "Here," he went on, "hold the shot like this. Get your whole weight behind it. That's right. Now, push with all the power you've got!"

This time the boy listened. When he tossed the shot, it went almost twice as far as before. "I guess you're right," he said with a grin.

In his senior year at college, Rafe was
elected president of the student body at
U.C.L.A. There was a lot for him to do.
"Rafe is about the best school president
we've ever had," students said. "He really
takes the job seriously."

Professors admired Rafe, too. "I trust
Rafer," said one of them. "I'd leave him
alone with the answers to tomorrow's test
and know he'd never peek."

And through all these activities, Rafe managed to keep up with his practice, working toward the 1960 Olympics. In 1958, he won the Nationals again. From there he went to Moscow for a special Russian-American track meet. It was the first time such a competition had ever been held.

Rafe, his mother, and Coach Drake arrive in Los Angeles where Rafe was guest of honor at a civic luncheon and dinner.

The Russian decathlon champion was Vasily Kuznetsov. Kuznetsov had come in third in the 1956 Olympics decathlon. But since then he had been getting better and better. In the spring of 1958, he had broken Rafe's world record.

"You'll just have to set a new one," friends told Rafe.

"I'll try," he promised with a laugh.

Rafe wins the 100-meter dash by a good margin. Vasily Kuznetsov of the Soviet Union is number 87.

Russian sports fans cheer Rafe in Moscow.

Rafe carried out that promise. In Moscow, he won the decathlon meet and set a new world's record. He also charmed the Russian people. They loved him, even though he had defeated their hero, Kuznetsov. They poured out of the stands and crowded around Rafe. They cheered him. They pressed flowers into his hands. No other American athlete had ever been so honored.

But setting a world's record was not the same as winning an Olympic gold medal. It was the gold medal that Rafe had set his heart on. And back home, a new rival had appeared on the scene.

He was Chuan-Kwang Yang, a young decathlon man from Nationalist China. "My government sent me here to your college to train," Yang told Rafe. "They said I was to keep an eye on you. You are the man I have to beat in 1960."

The two young athletes exchanged grins. They were from opposite sides of the world, but they could share a joke.

"You're going to beat me?" Rafe came back laughing. "Man you've got a long way to go!"

They told each other about their record speeds and distances. The Chinese boy was good. There was no doubt about that. He was lighter than Rafe which gave him an advantage in jumping and in the long races. "I'm going to catch up with you in the other events, too, Rafe," Yang promised.

"Well, now, let's see," said Rafe. He picked up a discus and sent the plate spinning down the field. "Let's see you beat that!" he told Yang with a grin.

The Chinese boy laughed and took his turn. It was the beginning of a long rivalry, friendly but fierce.

Rafe was also looking forward to competing in Philadelphia against an older rival, Vasily Kuznetsov of Russia.

But a couple of weeks before the meet, the worst happened. Rafe and his brother Jim were driving home to Kingsburg to attend their sister's high school graduation. Jim was driving. Rafe had just dozed off when Jim cried, "Watch out!" Jim quickly jammed on the brakes, but it was too late to avoid an accident.

Rafe felt the car wrench sharply, to avoid an oncoming car. Then there was a thundering crash. By the time rescue workers arrived, Rafe knew that his back was injured.

It was a sad moment for Rafer Johnson. He might never be able to compete in the decathlon again. His years of hard work, his years of dreaming might all be lost.

But Rafe did not give up hope. He was a graduate student now. Soon he would be qualified to teach. Teaching and helping people were important to him, too.

It was eight long months before Rafe was strong enough to train again.

Yang watched him take one of his first slow, painful jogs around the track. "You've still got what it takes, Rafe," he said with admiration.

And Rafe noticed that Yang was much better than he remembered.

Rafe shows how to take a hurdle.

It was February 1960. Now the Olympic Games were only five months away. As Rafe gained strength, he began to step up his decathlon practice, driving himself hard to get back in shape. Even with the help of his college coach, Elvin Drake, could he still make it?

"That Rafe Johnson," friends said, shaking their heads. "He's going to win the gold medal or kill himself trying."

The 1960 Olympics were held in Rome. On opening day, there was a grand parade of all the athletes from all the competing nations. The team from each country was led by a flagbearer chosen from its members.

"The honor of carrying the American flag," it was announced by the U.S. Olympic Committee, "will go to Rafer Johnson. Mr. Johnson is an athlete of world renown. He is also a young man of the highest character."

Rafe's 304 teammates cheered.

The big day dawned, sunny and beautiful. Rome was crowded with visitors. Flags were flying. Excitement was in the air.

More than 4,000 athletes took part in the Olympics parade. Spectators cheered as athletes filed into the stadium, nation by nation. The American group was near the end of the parade. Proudly Rafe lifted the Stars and Stripes and took his place. He led his countrymen into the great stadium.

They marched around the oval, Rafe in the lead. Then they stood with the other athletes and watched the opening ceremonies. Speeches were made. The Olympic torch was lighted. The 1960 Olympic Games were under way.

This was Rafe's big chance.

It was several days before the decathlon began. By then the weather had changed. Cold rain fell. The starting blocks for the 400-meter were under water.

After three events, officials stopped the meet. It was raining too hard. Hours passed. Then, when competition was started again, there were more delays. It was eleven at night before the day was over.

Rafe went to bed knowing he had a small lead.

"The tough part is still coming up," he said to a friend. "Yang is best at the pole vault and the 1,500."

He didn't sleep well that night. Would his dream come true or wouldn't it? The next day would tell.

The weather improved the following morning. There were few delays. But tension mounted with each event.

Yang won the high hurdles, Rafe won the discus. Yang won the pole vault, Rafe won the javelin throw. Before the final event, Rafe's lead was less than 100 points.

The 1,500-meter was announced. Rafe knew he would have to run his best. Yang had only to win the 1,500 by more than 10 yards. Then he could cut back Rafe's small point lead enough to win the meet. Both men were worn out, their legs shaky. Rafe was bigger than his rival, and perhaps it was worse for him.

Wearily, the men took their places. They tensed for the start. The gun went off, and Yang shot into the lead. Rafe fell in grimly right behind him.

On and on they raced. Rafe kept his eyes on his rival's back. He could not catch up and pass Yang, but he could keep him from increasing his lead.

The race seemed endless. Rafe drove himself on, never taking his eyes from his rival. Then, in the stretch, Yang put on a burst of speed. He started pulling away, three yards, four yards, five yards.

Rafe had come a long way for this moment. He had started out in a boxcar home in Kingsburg, California. His parents had dreamed, and so had he. He had worked hard and long. He could not let that victory escape him now. Pumping his weary legs, he closed the gap inch by inch by inch.

And there was the finish line. Yang swept across it. Four yards behind him came Rafer Lewis Johnson.

Rafe slowed down, catching his breath. He had won the big one. Years of hard work had made his dream come true. It was hard to realize at first. Then he heard the roar of the crowd.

Rafe turned to Yang, holding out his hand. "I only have 58 points to spare," he panted. "That's practically a tie."

Yang shook his head. "No, Rafe, you won," he said. "And you deserve to win."

The following day the awards were given out. At long last the precious gold medal was Rafe's.

After the ceremony, he was asked what his plans were for the future. He announced that he was giving up the decathlon.

"I love track and field," he said. "But there are other things in life, too."

Rafe's years of effort and practice are at last rewarded with the Olympic gold medal.

"What sort of things do you want to do, Rafe?" he was asked.

"I'm going to help people. I don't know how yet. But I'll find a way."

In the meantime, Rafe received movie and TV offers. He liked acting and making films and personal appearances. He also liked broadcasting. But Rafe still wanted to help people.

His chance came when the Peace Corps was formed. He was among the first volunteers. He became one of the State

Department's best representatives. At their request, he traveled to more than fifty different countries all over the world. In 1961, he toured the Near East. Then he went to Israel for the Maccabiah Games, an international Jewish competition. He served as coach and adviser to foreign teams.

"Governments can't really make people understand one another," he confided to a friend. "Only people can do that."

So, in 1962, he added another job to the ones he already had. He joined the movement known as People-to-People. One of the many activities of this movement is working with students. It helps young Americans make friendly contacts with foreign students in this country and in other countries of the world. Rafe was appointed West Coast Director of this organization.

The French Académie des Sports award for "Athlete of the Year" goes to Rafe in 1961. With Rafe are Sanford Marlowe (right) and Robert F. Kennedy.

"That Rafe Johnson," said admiring friends. "He just can't stop working."

No, he couldn't. But it was hard work that had won Rafer his gold medal. Now, surely, hard work would make him a champion in other fields.

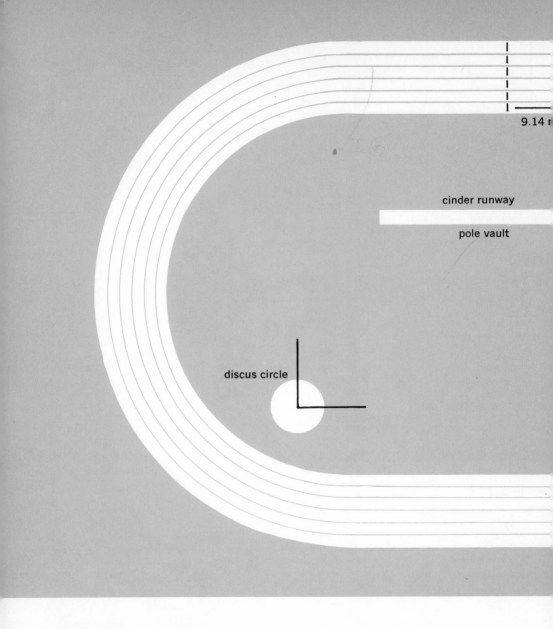

9.14 r

cinder runway

pole vault

discus circle

TRACK AND FIELD LAYOUT

This is a typical track and field layout where the Decathlon events take place. The running track is usually one-fourth of a mile in length and from 18 to 32 feet wide. Track and field events are some-times held indoors. On an indoor track the surface is usually of dirt or boards instead of cinders.

The full length of the track is used for the long races and only the straight part at the top for the short ones.

The pole used in vaulting is made of steel or fiber glass. It is 12 to 16 feet in length.